The
BASEBALL STADIUM
Postcard Album

31 Postcards of American League Ballparks

By
Michael Gershman

Produced by Michael Gershman for Sports Extra, Inc.
Taylor Publishing Company
Dallas, Texas

Author's Note

Most of the cards in this album were taken from the collection of Gavin Riley, who graciously allowed them to be photographed. I must also thank the Metropolitan Toronto Convention and Visitors Association for allowing me to use the card of the Skydome. Postcards are arranged alphabetically by team name — Angels, Athletics, Blue Jays, Brewers, Browns, Indians, Mariners, Orioles, Rangers, Red Sox, Royals, Senators, Tigers, Twins, White Sox, Yankees.

© 1990 Michael Gershman

Cover Photo — League Park, Cleveland
Cover tinting and design by Michael A. Schacht

Published by Taylor Publishing Company
1550 West Mockingbird Lane
Dallas, Texas 75235
First printing
Printed in Singapore
ISBN 0-87833-697-4

NEWEST AND FINEST IN THE UNITED STATES

106685

Wrigley Field (Los Angeles) Originally a Pacific Coast League park and the site of TV's "Home Run Derby," Wrigley hosted the Angels only in 1961. A major league record was set that season for most homers hit in one park (245).

The Baseball Stadium Postcard Album (American League Edition)
© 1990 by Michael Gershman. Published by Taylor Publishing Co.

Anaheim, California　　　　　　　　　　　*California Angels' Stadium*

Anaheim Stadium The Angels got their own park in April 1966. It was nicknamed "the Big A" both for Anaheim and for the 230-foot halo-circled "A" which helped support the scoreboard until 1980, when it was moved to the parking lot.

The Baseball Stadium Postcard Album (American League Edition)
© 1990 by Michael Gershman. Published by Taylor Publishing Co.

COLUMBIA BALL PARK, PHILADELPHIA, PA.

Columbia Park (Philadelphia) Connie Mack's Athletics occupied this wooden park located in the Brewerytown section from 1901 to 1908. The A's played two World Series games here in 1905 and were shut out both times by Christy Mathewson.

The Baseball Stadium Postcard Album (American League Edition)
© 1990 by Michael Gershman. Published by Taylor Publishing Co.

Connie Mack Stadium

Shibe Park (Philadelphia)   Shibe, later Connie Mack Stadium, was home for Mack's Athletics from 1909 to 1954. Ted Williams went 6 for 8 in a doubleheader here to end 1941 as the major leagues' last .400 hitter (.406).

The Baseball Stadium Postcard Album (American League Edition)
© 1990 by Michael Gershman. Published by Taylor Publishing Co.

53:—MUEHLEBACH FIELD, KANSAS CITY, MO.

Municipal Stadium (Kansas City) Muehlebach Field (Ruppert Stadium, Blues Stadium) became Municipal Stadium when the A's moved here in 1955. The old Braves Field scoreboard in right center was located next to Charlie Finley's goats and sheep.

The Baseball Stadium Postcard Album (American League Edition)
© 1990 by Michael Gershman. Published by Taylor Publishing Co.

Oakland-Alameda County Stadium   Less than a month after the A's moved here in 1968, Catfish Hunter threw a perfect game against the Twins. The huge foul territory, largest in the majors, reduces batting averages by five to seven points.

The Baseball Stadium Postcard Album (American League Edition)
© 1990 by Michael Gershman. Published by Taylor Publishing Co.

TORONTO

Exhibition Stadium (Toronto)   The home of the Canadian Football League Argonauts, Exhibition Stadium served as the Blue Jays' home from 1977 to 1989. It is the only park in which a game was called off because of wind (April 30, 1984).

The Baseball Stadium Postcard Album (American League Edition)
© 1990 by Michael Gershman. Published by Taylor Publishing Co.

Skydome (Toronto)   The first baseball stadium built with a fully retractable roof opened June 5, 1989 as the Brewers beat the Blue Jays, 5-3. The roof encompasses an area of eight acres and, when closed, is 282 feet high.

The Baseball Stadium Postcard Album (American League Edition)
© 1990 by Michael Gershman. Published by Taylor Publishing Co.

Sick's Stadium (Seattle) Named after PCL Seattle Indians' president Emil Sick, Sick's hosted the Pilots in their only year of existence (1969). On Opening Day, 700 fans waited patiently while carpenters finished building their seats.

The Baseball Stadium Postcard Album (American League Edition)
© 1990 by Michael Gershman. Published by Taylor Publishing Co.

County Stadium (Milwaukee) The first park built with public money, County Stadium hosted the Braves from 1953 to 1965 and the White Sox (for 20 "home" games) in 1968 and 1969. The transplanted Pilots became the Brewers in 1970.

The Baseball Stadium Postcard Album (American League Edition)
© 1990 by Michael Gershman. Published by Taylor Publishing Co.

SPORTSMEN'S PARK, ST. LOUIS, MO.—98

Sportsman's Park (St. Louis)   A diamond was laid out here in 1866, and the Browns won four straight American Association championships here (1885 to 1888). On August 19, 1951, 43-inch-high Eddie Gaedel walked on four pitches.

The Baseball Stadium Postcard Album (American League Edition)
© 1990 by Michael Gershman. Published by Taylor Publishing Co.

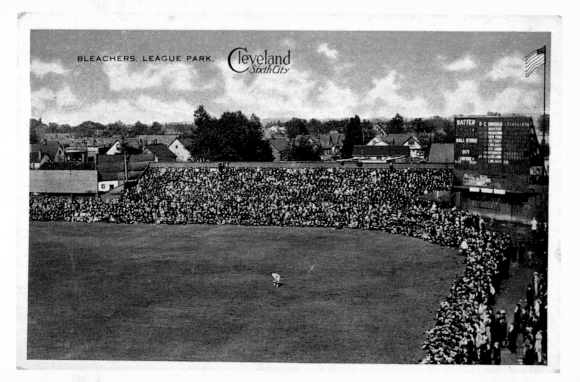

BLEACHERS, LEAGUE PARK. Cleveland Sixth City

League Park (Cleveland)   Home to the Indians from 1910 to 1932 and weekdays from 1934 to 1946, the park's weird angles had left fielders chasing balls in right. Joe DiMaggio's 56-game hitting streak ended here on July 16, 1941.

The Baseball Stadium Postcard Album (American League Edition)
© 1990 by Michael Gershman. Published by Taylor Publishing Co.

Cleveland Municipal Stadium, Cleveland, Ohio

Cleveland Stadium The Indians first played at what was then Lakefront Stadium on July 31, 1932. Known as Municipal Stadium in the 1940s and 1950s, it hosted the largest crowd in AL history (84,857) on September 12, 1954.

The Baseball Stadium Postcard Album (American League Edition)
© 1990 by Michael Gershman. Published by Taylor Publishing Co.

Kingdome (Seattle) The Kingdome opened April 6, 1977. It hasn't been homer-prone like other domed stadiums, because forty-two air conditioners blow air towards home plate. On May 6, 1982 Gaylord Perry won his 300th game here.

The Baseball Stadium Postcard Album (American League Edition)
© 1990 by Michael Gershman. Published by Taylor Publishing Co.

Memorial Stadium, Baltimore

Memorial Stadium (Baltimore)   Memorial opened on April 15, 1954, and its upper deck has remained open ever since. Frank Robinson hit the only fair ball out of the stadium on May 8, 1966, and a flag reading "Here" marks the spot.

The Baseball Stadium Postcard Album (American League Edition)
© 1990 by Michael Gershman. Published by Taylor Publishing Co.

Arlington Stadium Built in 1965 for the Texas League Dallas-Fort Worth Spurs, Turnpike Stadium became Arlington Stadium and the Rangers' home on April 21, 1972. Since it's the warmest park in the majors, balls carry well here.

The Baseball Stadium Postcard Album (American League Edition)
© 1990 by Michael Gershman. Published by Taylor Publishing Co.

Huntington Avenue Grounds (Boston) Huntington hosted the Pilgrims (Red Sox) from 1901 to 1911. It was the site of both the first World Series game in 1903 and the first modern perfect game, pitched by Cy Young on May 5, 1904.

Fenway Park (Boston) The Green Monster in left field is one reason Fenway produces 13 percent more offense than other parks. After the 1975 season, the original green sheet metal was cut up and sold for contributions to the Jimmy Fund.

The Baseball Stadium Postcard Album (American League Edition)
© 1990 by Michael Gershman. Published by Taylor Publishing Co.

Royals Stadium (Kansas City) Royals Stadium, part of the
Harry S. Truman Complex along with the Chiefs' Arrowhead
Stadium, opened on April 10, 1973. Less than six weeks later,
on May 15th, Nolan Ryan pitched his first no-hitter here.

The Baseball Stadium Postcard Album (American League Edition)
© 1990 by Michael Gershman. Published by Taylor Publishing Co.

GRIFFITH STADIUM OPENING DAY

Griffith Stadium (Washington) Griffith, built on the site of American League Park, hosted the Senators, who were "first in war, first in peace, and last in the American League" until October 10, 1924, when Walter Johnson's team became champions.

The Baseball Stadium Postcard Album (American League Edition)
© 1990 by Michael Gershman. Published by Taylor Publishing Co.

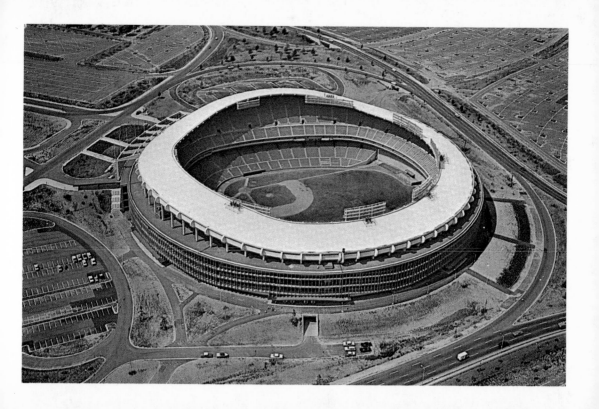

RFK Stadium (Washington)   President Kennedy threw out the first ball at D.C. Stadium, home of the expansion Senators, on April 2, 1962. Renamed Robert F. Kennedy Memorial Stadium in 1969, it was the Senators' home base until 1971.

The Baseball Stadium Postcard Album (American League Edition)
© 1990 by Michael Gershman. Published by Taylor Publishing Co.

Detroit Baseball Team, having a Flag Day at the Season's Opening, Detroit, Mich.

Navin Field (Detroit)   The Tigers have played every home game at what was originally Bennett Park. On April 20, 1912, it was renamed after owner Frank Navin, and, in the first inning, Ty Cobb stole home on the front end of a double steal.

The Baseball Stadium Postcard Album (American League Edition)
© 1990 by Michael Gershman. Published by Taylor Publishing Co.

Tiger Stadium at All Star Time

Tiger Stadium (Detroit) Renamed Briggs Stadium in 1938, it was the last American League park to install lights (June 15, 1948). Dubbed Tiger Stadium in 1961, the park recalls its heroes with streets named Kaline Drive and Cochrane Avenue.

The Baseball Stadium Postcard Album (American League Edition)
© 1990 by Michael Gershman. Published by Taylor Publishing Co.

Metropolitan Stadium (Minneapolis)   The minor league Millers played here until the Twins took over in 1961. Harmon Killebrew and Bob Allison became the first teammates to hit grand slams in the same inning here on July 18, 1962.

The Baseball Stadium Postcard Album (American League Edition)
© 1990 by Michael Gershman. Published by Taylor Publishing Co.

Metrodome (Minneapolis)   The Hubert H. Humphrey Metrodome opened April 6, 1982, and Twins fans set noise records during the 1987 World Series. On May 4, 1984, Dave Kingman hit a ball through the roof which never came down; it was ruled a double.

The Baseball Stadium Postcard Album (American League Edition)
© 1990 by Michael Gershman. Published by Taylor Publishing Co.

SOUTH SIDE BALL PARK, CHICAGO, WHITE SOX

South Side Park (Chicago)   The site of the Chicago Cricket
Club was the White Sox home from April 1901 until June 1910.
The Sox won the first American League pennant in 1901 and
took the 1906 World Series here with an 8-3 win over the Cubs.

The Baseball Stadium Postcard Album (American League Edition)
© 1990 by Michael Gershman. Published by Taylor Publishing Co.

Comiskey Park (Chicago) Blessed with a green cornerstone laid on St. Patrick's Day in 1910, Charles A. Comiskey's Baseball Palace of the World was the Cubs' home park for the 1918 World Series and hosted the first All-Star Game.

The Baseball Stadium Postcard Album (American League Edition)
© 1990 by Michael Gershman. Published by Taylor Publishing Co.

Comiskey Park (Chicago)   When Bill Veeck took over the Sox, he had the cornerstone painted white and brought a pennant (1959), baseball's first exploding scoreboard (1960), and its last Disco Demolition Night on July 12, 1979.

The Baseball Stadium Postcard Album (American League Edition)
© 1990 by Michael Gershman. Published by Taylor Publishing Co.

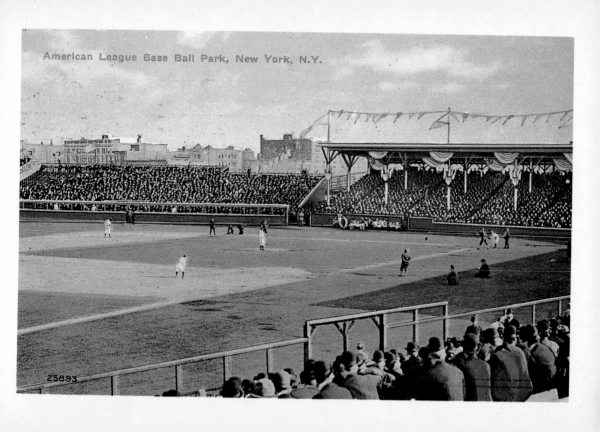

American League Base Ball Park, New York, N.Y.

25893

Hilltop Park (New York) The Highlanders (Yankees) played their first home game at Hilltop Park on April 30, 1903. In 1911, the Giants played here when the Polo Grounds burned.

The Baseball Stadium Postcard Album (American League Edition)
© 1990 by Michael Gershman. Published by Taylor Publishing Co.

Yankee Stadium (New York)   The House That Ruth Built
opened, fittingly, with a Ruth home run on April 18, 1923. The
Bronx Bombers won their first championship that year and
added twenty others before the Stadium was rebuilt in 1974.

The Baseball Stadium Postcard Album (American League Edition)
© 1990 by Michael Gershman. Published by Taylor Publishing Co.

The "New" Yankee Stadium - Bronx, N.Y.

Yankee Stadium (New York) The Yanks played two years at Shea, reopened the Stadium April 15, 1976, and won the pennant but were swept by the Reds. On October 18, 1977, Reggie Jackson's three home runs won Game 6 and the Series.

The Baseball Stadium Postcard Album (American League Edition)
© 1990 by Michael Gershman. Published by Taylor Publishing Co.